# NATIONAL PLAN TO ACHIEVE MARITIME DOMAIN AWARENESS

## FOR
### THE NATIONAL STRATEGY FOR MARITIME SECURITY

OCTOBER 2005

# FOREWORD

By signing National Security Presidential Directive-41/Homeland Security Presidential Directive-13 (NSPD-41/HSPD-13) (Maritime Security Policy, December 21, 2004) President Bush underscored the importance of securing the Maritime Domain, which is defined as *"All areas and things of, on, under, relating to, adjacent to, or bordering on a sea, ocean, or other navigable waterway, including all maritime-related activities, infrastructure, people, cargo, and vessels and other conveyances."* NSPD-41/HSPD-13 established a Maritime Security Policy Coordinating Committee—the first coordinating committee tasked specifically to address this issue—to oversee the development of a National Strategy for Maritime Security and eight supporting implementation plans:

- **National Plan to Achieve Maritime Domain Awareness** lays the foundation for an effective understanding of anything associated with the Maritime Domain that could impact the security, safety, economy, or environment of the United States and identifying threats as early and as distant from our shores as possible.

- **Global Maritime Intelligence Integration Plan** uses existing capabilities to integrate all available intelligence regarding potential threats to U.S. interests in the Maritime Domain.

- **Maritime Operational Threat Response Plan** aims for coordinated U.S. Government response to threats against the United States and its interests in the Maritime Domain by establishing roles and responsibilities, which enable the government to respond quickly and decisively.

- **International Outreach and Coordination Strategy** provides a framework to coordinate all maritime security initiatives undertaken with foreign governments and international organizations, and solicits international support for enhanced maritime security.

- **Maritime Infrastructure Recovery Plan** recommends procedures and standards for the recovery of the maritime infrastructure following attack or similar disruption.

- **Maritime Transportation System Security Plan** responds to the President's call for recommendations to improve the national and international regulatory framework regarding the maritime domain.

- **Maritime Commerce Security Plan** establishes a comprehensive plan to secure the maritime supply chain.

- **Domestic Outreach Plan** engages non-Federal input to assist with the development and implementation of maritime security policies resulting from NSPD-41/HSPD-13.

Although these plans address different aspects of maritime security, they are mutually linked and reinforce each other. Together, the National Strategy for Maritime Security and its supporting plans represent a comprehensive national effort to enhance the security of the United States by preventing hostile or illegal acts within the Maritime Domain.

These plans do not alter existing constitutional or statutory authorities or responsibilities of the department and agency heads to carry out operational activities or to provide or receive information.

# EXECUTIVE SUMMARY

"The heart of the Maritime Domain Awareness program is accurate information, intelligence, surveillance, and reconnaissance of all vessels, cargo, and people extending well beyond our traditional maritime boundaries."

PRESIDENT BUSH
JANUARY 20, 2002

Maritime Domain Awareness (MDA) is the effective understanding of anything associated with the global maritime domain that could impact the security, safety, economy, or environment of the United States. MDA is a key component of an active, layered maritime defense in depth. It will be achieved by improving our ability to collect, fuse, analyze, display, and disseminate actionable information and intelligence to operational commanders. MDA is supported by the *Global Maritime Intelligence Integration Plan* and is the enabler for the *Maritime Operational Threat Response Plan.*

This plan advocates enhanced and innovative collection of intelligence, the integration of correlated open source information, and the incorporation of automated algorithms to assist human analytic efforts. The National Maritime Intelligence Center will be the central point of connectivity to fuse, analyze, and disseminate information and intelligence for shared situational awareness across classification boundaries.

To achieve persistent awareness in the maritime domain, Cold War legacy collection capabilities alone are no longer sufficient. We must reorient and integrate these legacy systems with current and emerging capabilities, such as unmanned aerial vehicles and acoustic sensors, fused in a common operating picture available to maritime operational commanders and accessible throughout the United States Government. Employment of these collection capabilities will maximize near-real time awareness of maritime threats.

Stand-off detection capabilities for weapons of mass destruction in the maritime domain must be developed to complement existing and emerging cargo inspection systems and hand-held detection devices. Most significantly, human intelligence collection and the investigative actions of law enforcement officers can provide crucial insights about maritime threats.

The primary method for information sharing, situational awareness, and collaborative planning will be the national maritime common operating picture (COP). The COP is a near-real time, dynamically tailorable, network-centric virtual information grid shared by all U.S. Federal, state, and local agencies with maritime interests and responsibilities. COP data will be accessible to all users, except when limited by security, policy, or regulations.

Successful execution of this plan requires a sustained and adaptive national effort. Critical to this effort is the coordination and collaboration of the Federal, state, local, tribal and international partners as well as the private sector. An Implementation Team is established to implement this Plan and follow-on MDA supporting plans. Ultimately, the backbone of protecting the United States from maritime threats is an active, layered defense. MDA is the critical link to achieving this effective defense through persistent awareness and decision superiority. The *National Plan to Achieve Maritime Domain Awareness* will make the United States more secure.

# TABLE OF CONTENTS

# I.  CONTEXT

Seafarers have sought an understanding of the oceans for centuries.  The United States has relied upon technology to collect data in this environment.  Today's complex and ambiguous threats place an even greater premium on knowledge and a shared understanding of the maritime domain.  Adequately addressing these threats requires effective and superior decision-making.  Decision superiority is enabled by ensuring global maritime information dominance through the collection, integration and dissemination of information and intelligence, and the development of knowledge.  An effective understanding of the global maritime domain enables focused law enforcement and military action, supports strategic decision-making and operational threat response while promoting freedom, civil liberties, and prosperity for all.  This Plan supports the strategic objectives and elements of the National Strategy for Maritime Security (NSMS), which emphasizes **"the ability to know, so that preemptive or interdiction actions may be taken as early as possible."**  In addition, implementing this plan directly supports the Global Maritime Intelligence Integration and Maritime Operational Threat Response Plans tasked by the Presidential Directive on Maritime Security Policy (NSPD-41/HSPD-13).

## PURPOSE OF THE PLAN

The *National Plan to Achieve Maritime Domain Awareness* is a cornerstone for successful execution of the security plans tasked in NSPD-41/HSPD-13.  This Plan serves to unify United States Government and support international efforts to achieve MDA across the Federal government, with the private sector and civil authorities within the United States, and with our allies and partners.  It directs close coordination of a broad range of federal departments and agencies for this lasting endeavor.  Implementation of this Plan will be conducted under the oversight of an interagency implementation team.

## KEY DEFINITIONS

**Maritime Domain** is all areas and things of, on, under, relating to, adjacent to, or bordering on a sea, ocean, or other navigable waterway, including all maritime related activities, infrastructure, people, cargo, and vessels and other conveyances.

**Maritime Domain Awareness** is the effective understanding of anything associated with the maritime domain that could impact the security, safety, economy, or environment of the United States.

**Global Maritime Community of Interest** (GMCOI) includes, among other interests, the federal, state, and local departments and agencies with responsibilities in the maritime domain.  Because certain risks and interests are common to government, business, and citizen alike, community membership also includes public, private and commercial stakeholders, as well as foreign governments and international stakeholders.

There are few areas of greater strategic importance than the maritime domain. The oceans are global thoroughfares that sustain our national prosperity and are vital for our national security. Distinct from other domains (e.g., air and space), the maritime domain provides an expansive pathway through the global commons. Terrorist organizations recognize this, and also realize the importance of exploiting the maritime domain for financial gain and movement of equipment and personnel, as well as a medium for launching attacks. The maritime domain presents a broad array of potential targets that fit terrorists' operational objectives of achieving mass casualties and inflicting economic harm.

The basis for effective prevention measures is awareness and threat knowledge, along with credible deterrent and interdiction capabilities. Without effective understanding of maritime domain activities, gained through persistent awareness, vital opportunities for an early response can be lost. Awareness grants time and distance to detect, deter, interdict, and defeat adversaries. The maritime threat environment of the 21$^{st}$ Century requires broader scope and a more comprehensive vision. We must look beyond traditional surveillance of ports, waterways, and oceans, and continuously adapt to new challenges and opportunities. We must set priorities for existing and developing capabilities to efficiently minimize risks while contending with an uncertain future. Our understanding of the maritime domain must incorporate intelligence originally acquired in overseas land areas and domestic law enforcement and intelligence information. MDA provides operational maritime commanders a near-real time ability to defeat hostile nation and transnational terrorist threats.

## MDA Goals

MDA supports core national defense and security priorities over the next decade. MDA serves to simplify today's complex and ambiguous security environment by meeting the following strategic goals:

- **Enhance transparency in the maritime domain to detect, deter and defeat threats as early and distant from U.S. interests as possible;**

- **Enable accurate, dynamic, and confident decisions and responses to the full spectrum of maritime threats; and**

- **Sustain the full application of the law to ensure freedom of navigation and the efficient flow of commerce.**

## MDA Objectives

Achieving MDA depends on the ability to monitor activities in such a way that trends can be identified and anomalies differentiated. Data alone are insufficient. Data must be collected, fused, and analyzed, preferably with the assistance of computer data integration and analysis algorithms to assist in handling vast, disparate data streams, so that operational decision makers can anticipate threats and take the initiative to defeat them. The following objectives constitute the MDA Essential Task List, which will guide the development of capabilities that the United States Government will pursue and when executed will provide the GMCOI an effective understanding of the maritime domain.

- **Persistently monitor in the global maritime domain:**
  - **Vessels and craft**
  - **Cargo**
  - **Vessel crews and passengers**
  - **All identified areas of interest**
- **Access and maintain data on vessels, facilities, and infrastructure**
- **Collect, fuse, analyze, and disseminate information to decision makers to facilitate effective understanding.**
- **Access, develop and maintain data on MDA-related mission performance.**

**Persistently Monitor** The integrated management of a diverse set of collection and processing capabilities, operated to detect and understand the activity of interest with sufficient sensor dwell, revisit rate, and required quality to expeditiously assess adversary actions, predict adversary plans, deny sanctuary to an adversary, and assess results of U.S./coalition actions. "Persistently monitor" in this Plan refers to an ability to conduct persistent monitoring anywhere on the globe. It is not meant to imply that we can simultaneously do persistent monitoring over the entire globe.

Achieving the essential tasks will make MDA the critical enabler for national maritime security and enable effective decision-making for United States Government maritime operational threat responses. The pursuit of the goals and objectives outlined above will be guided by the following principles and assumptions.

**Guiding Principles**

**The first step towards meeting these principles is to ensure GMCOI stakeholders, at all levels, know what they can do to help, how they can do it and, most importantly why Maritime Domain Awareness is in their collective best interest. The openness of American society and the structure of our traditional governance argue against**

**centralizing all aspects of MDA within an expanded federal infrastructure. However, it will demand a common purpose and agreed upon procedures.**

**Unity of Effort.** MDA requires a coordinated effort within and among the GMCOI, including public and private sector organizations, and international partners. The need for security is a mutual interest requiring the cooperation of industry and government.

**Information Sharing and Integration.** MDA depends upon unparalleled information sharing. MDA must have protocols to protect private sector proprietary information. Bilateral or multilateral information sharing agreements and international conventions and treaties will be MDA enablers.

The primary method for information sharing is the national maritime common operational picture (COP). The COP is a near-time, dynamically tailorable, network-centric virtual information grid shared by all U.S. Federal, state, and local agencies with maritime interests and responsibilities. COP data will be accessible to all users, except when limited by security, policy, or regulations. The COP also contains decision-maker toolsets fed by one or more distributed and exchanged object and track databases to facilitate collaborative planning and assist all echelons in achieving situational awareness. Each user can filter and contribute to these databases according to his or her information needs, responsibilities, and level of access.

**Safe and Efficient Flow of Commerce.** Public safety and economic security are mutually reinforcing. All members of the GMCOI must recognize that the safe and efficient flow of commerce is enhanced and harmonized by an effective understanding of the maritime domain. The converse is also true, that MDA is enhanced by responsible participation in an accountable system of commerce. The two concepts are mutually reinforcing.

## Planning Assumptions

The Plan makes the following assumptions:

- Federal, state, local, tribal, private sector, and international partners will participate;

- Existing systems and capabilities will be leveraged and integrated;

- The need for security will be harmonized with the imperative to preserve fundamental liberties, freedom of navigation, and the legitimate use of the seas for commercial and recreational purposes;

- All maritime stakeholders will take a collaborative approach to establish unprecedented information exchange and pooling of resources; and

- International participation in maritime security activities including information sharing with other states or acting against threats remains voluntary for each nation.

**Threats**

The variety of maritime domain threats include:

- ***Nation-State Threats.*** The prospect of major regional conflicts erupting, escalating, and drawing in major powers should not be discounted. Nonetheless, for the near-term, states represent a more significant challenge to global security. Some states of concern provide safe havens for criminals and terrorists, who use these countries as bases of operations to export illicit activities into the maritime domain and into other areas of the globe. The probability of a rogue government using a WMD is expected to increase during the next decade. An even greater danger is that a state of concern will provide critical advanced conventional weaponry, WMD components, delivery systems and related materials, technologies and weapons expertise to another rogue state or a terrorist organization that is willing to conduct WMD attacks. This is of the greatest concern since the maritime domain is the likely venue by which WMD will be brought into the United States.

- ***Terrorist Threats.*** The vastness of the maritime domain provides great opportunities for exploitation by terrorists. The use of smaller commercial and recreational vessels closer to our shores and areas of interest to transport WMD/E is of significant concern. Additionally, terrorists can use large merchant ships to move powerful conventional explosives or WMD/E for detonation in a port or alongside an offshore facility. Terrorist groups have demonstrated a capacity to use shipping as a means of conveyance for positioning their agents, logistics support, and revenue generation. Terrorists have shown that they have the capability to use explosives-laden suicide boats as weapons. This capability could easily be used with merchant ships as kinetic weapons to ram another vessel, warship, port facility, or offshore platforms.

- ***Transnational Criminal and Piracy Threats.*** Modern-day pirates and other criminals are well organized and well equipped, often possessing advanced communications, weapons, and high-speed craft to conduct smuggling of people, drugs, weapons, and other contraband, as well as piracy.

- ***Environmental and Social Threats.*** Catastrophic destruction of marine resources, conflict between nation-states over maritime resources, and mass migration flows have the potential to harm the maritime domain or destabilize regions of the world. The accompanying economic impacts are often significant.

KEY ORGANIZATIONS

**Governmental Organizations**

The Maritime Security Policy Coordinating Committee (MSPCC), established by NSPD-41/HSPD-13 and co-chaired by representatives from the NSC and HSC staffs, is the primary forum for coordinating and implementing policies, strategies, and initiatives of this plan. Both through the MSPCC and other organizational implementation efforts, the

United States Government will work with relevant intergovernmental, state, and local agencies, as well as private sector and international partners, to execute this plan.

## International Organizations

MDA must be embedded into all maritime activities to enhance global maritime security. Close, continual cooperation with international organizations is required to achieve MDA. For example, the International Maritime Organization (IMO) took steps toward embedding security within the global maritime domain with the adoption of the International Ship and Port Facility Security (ISPS) code. This provides a standardized, consistent framework for evaluating risk, enabling governments to offset changes in threat with changes in vulnerability for ships and port facilities. To help facilitate global MDA, this plan will leverage the efforts of the NSMS International Outreach and Coordination Strategy, which provides a framework to coordinate all maritime security initiatives undertaken with foreign governments and international organizations, and solicits international support for enhanced maritime security.

## Private Sector Organizations

Initiatives conducted with the support of the private sector are also necessary to ensure full information dominance in the maritime domain. Public-private sector partnership initiatives, such as the Customs-Trade Partnership Against Terrorism (C-TPAT), provide models for enhancing awareness and incentives for private sector participation. Such initiatives have helped enhance the visibility and security of the global supply chain, a key element of MDA. To this end, we must engage private sector organizations to include: Harbor Safety Committees, shipping companies, associations and consortia within the GMCOI, including the National Maritime Security Advisory Committee (NMSAC) and other private sector advisory committees.

## II.  EFFECTIVE DECISION-MAKING

"America, in this new century, again faces new threats.  Instead of massed armies, we face stateless networks; we face killers who hide in our own cities.  We must confront deadly technologies.  To inflict great harm on our country, America's enemies need to be only right once.  Our intelligence and law enforcement professionals in our government must be right every single time."

PRESIDENT BUSH
DECEMBER 17, 2004

The purpose of MDA is to **facilitate timely, accurate decision-making**.  MDA does not direct actions, but enables them to be done more quickly and with precision.  MDA is achieved by (1) collecting, analyzing and disseminating data, information and intelligence to decision makers, and (2) applying functional and operational knowledge in the context of known and potential threats.  A United States Government MDA capability that is integrated, interoperable, and efficient, coupled with continually improving knowledge is required to meet today's mission requirements.  **Figure 1 demonstrates the interaction between capabilities, knowledge development, and their collective contribution to understanding and effective decision-making.**

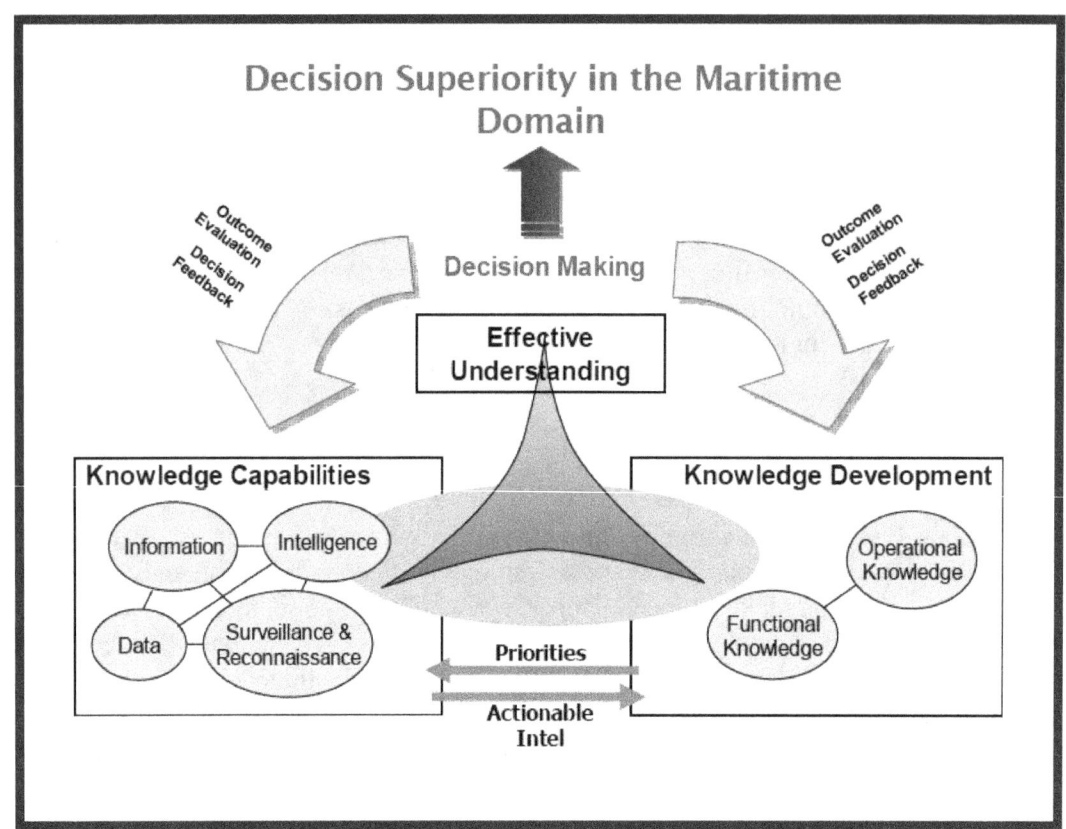

Figure 1

TERMS OF REFERENCE

**Data**.[1] Representation of facts, concepts, or instructions in a formalized manner suitable for communication, interpretation, or processing by humans or by automatic means. Any representations such as characters or analog quantities to which meaning is or might be assigned.

**Information**. Facts, data, or instructions in any medium or form. The meaning that a human assigns to data by means of the known conventions used in their representation.

**Intelligence**. The product resulting from the collection, processing, integration, analysis, evaluation, and interpretation of available information concerning foreign countries or areas. Information and knowledge about an adversary obtained through observation, investigation, analysis, or understanding.

**Knowledge**.[2] Familiarity or awareness gained through experience or study. The sum or range of what has been perceived, discovered, or learned.

---

[1] Definitions for Data, Information, and Intelligence adopted from the DoD Dictionary of Military and Associated Terms (Joint Pub 1-02)

[2] Definition for Knowledge adopted from the Joint Forces Command (JFCOM) Glossary of Terms

**Understanding.** Ability to comprehend the sense or meaning of something based on the application of knowledge against data, information, and intelligence.

**By delivering these elements in a manner quickly and easily comprehended**, MDA shortens decision cycles and enables decisive operational response.

KNOWLEDGE CAPABILITIES

Understanding the maritime domain will result from the employment of traditional intelligence capabilities and processes fed by, and synchronized with, operational decision-making processes. The collection, fusion, analysis and dissemination of prioritized categories of maritime intelligence and all-source information are the fundamental building blocks of MDA.

The global maritime domain includes a wide variety of interlocking and connected systems operating within, adjacent to and beyond the physical oceans and waterways that must be brought into better focus. Detecting and interdicting threats within a system that crosses domestic and international jurisdictions requires a persistent awareness. **Intelligence, Surveillance and Reconnaissance (ISR) capabilities are required in a layered approach that provides more comprehensive awareness of threats and illegal activities as they approach the United States.**

Achieving MDA requires integration of data, information and intelligence from a broad range of sources, categorized as follows:

- **Vessels**—characteristics such as flag, type, tonnage, maximum speed, origin, and track
- **Cargo**—from a vessel's manifest, shipment origin, human intelligence (HUMINT), or as input from chemical/biological/nuclear/radiation/explosive detection sensors
- **Vessel crews and passengers**—to include crew, dockworkers, and passengers
- **Maritime Areas of Interest**—a focusing of surveillance capabilities to particular geographic points such as sea lanes or oceanic regions
- **Ports**, waterways, and facilities - port terminals, piers, cranes, petrol facilities, and other characteristics
- **The Environment** - weather, currents, natural resources, fish stocks
- **Maritime Critical Infrastructure** – nuclear power plants, rail heads, transportation nodes, bridges, and undersea fiber optic cables and pipelines
- **Threats and Activities** - identified threats and inherently dangerous activities such as illegal migration, drug smuggling, or offshore drilling
- **Friendly Forces** – operational information on military, federal, state, local, and/or allied assets operating in the maritime domain
- **Financial Transactions** - illegal money trails, hidden vessel or cargo ownership

Of the above categories, priority is placed on the data, information, and intelligence associated with **people, cargo, and vessels engaged in maritime activities. The**

**potential for exploitation in these areas makes them the most critical priorities of information and intelligence collection.**

To meet emerging threats, MDA may be required to support the entire spectrum of national security events – from the Global War on Terrorism and stability operations to disaster response and recovery. These requirements may call for a surge or sustained capability to provide MDA where strategically, operationally, or tactically most important. In these cases, capabilities supporting MDA will be focused toward identified maritime areas of interest, such as military vessels or formations, the center of a maritime operating area or a geographic area of interest (e.g., choke point, special security events, sea lines of communication, strategic port, high threat area, etc.).

## KNOWLEDGE DEVELOPMENT

Knowledge capabilities alone will not ensure effective decision-making. Information and intelligence becomes actionable only when decision makers are equipped with knowledge and are positioned to act. Developing the ability to know, so that immediate or deliberate actions may be taken at the time and place of our choosing requires a dedicated and sustained effort to develop a dynamic knowledge base.

This Plan focuses on two critical pillars of knowledge development directed towards decision-making.

**Functional knowledge** is "expert" knowledge. Functional knowledge is gained primarily through traditional academic study. Experts assigned to a particular field or operating area possess this type of knowledge.

**Operational knowledge** is based on action and experience. Decision makers and supporting staffs gain this knowledge on the basis of situational experience learned through real-world case prosecution or effective exercise and training programs.

Knowledge development, particularly operational knowledge, depends on a continuous and active feedback mechanism. Each decision will have consequences and a desired outcome. These results must be evaluated and lessons applied to MDA priorities and capabilities, and knowledge development. Nowhere is the interaction with a broad cross-section of federal, state, public and private, and international partners more important than in the application of knowledge. Federal agencies must tap into the significant reservoirs of functional and operational knowledge at every echelon of decision-making in order to enhance their ability to make the right decisions at the right time. Initiatives such as virtual and established Lessons Learned Centers of Excellence as well as the development of training and exercise programs will be pursued. Doing so will help ensure the United States is positioned to take early and effective action against the entire spectrum of maritime threats. Figure 2 contains an example of knowledge development in action.

## UNDERSTANDING

Effective understanding is the synthesis of national capabilities and knowledge development that will produce the level of understanding required to insure effective decision-making. Priority must be placed on, and continually validated by decision maker requirements. The potential for MDA as a force multiplier by shortening decision cycles and enabling timely operational responses rests in its ability to deliver information in a manner useful and executable by decision makers.

**Knowledge Development**: U.S. embassy in Europe passes that an informant has reported an attempt to smuggle an improvised nuclear device (IND) on a cargo vessel enroute the United States. Some details such as the approximate date and probable port of debarkation are provided, but the vessel name and U.S. destination are unknown.

**Information**: A general service cargo vessel en route the United States files Electronic Notice of Arrival (ENOA) with USCG/CBP.

**Decision**: Senior U.S. officials decide that the threat is serious, and that government assets must identify, track, and interdict the vessel. DOD is given the lead to in accordance with the Maritime Operational Threat Response Plan.

**Operational Knowledge** of the threat is disseminated to the Global Maritime Community of Interest via COP. CBP readjusts targeting criteria to reflect the new threat. The Automated Targeting System (ATS) identifies an anomaly in the cargo manifest of the reporting vessel.

**Decision**: The National Targeting Center selects the vessel for further inspection and reviews the cargo manifest in detail as well as the crew/passenger list in the Advanced Passenger Information System. The vessel's Automated Information System (AIS) track in the COP is "flagged."

**Knowledge Capabilities**: Analysts determine there are 32 possible suspect vessels given the time frame and port of debarkation. Joint Operational Intelligence Center analysts note the flagged vessel had called at the port of debarkation in the correct time frame and designate the ship a VOI. Additional HUMINT validates that the VOI is indeed suspect and national assets are refocused to verify VOI's location.

**Knowledge**: COP reveals the closest asset capable of at-sea interdiction is a Coast Guard cutter on routine operations. CBP asks carrier, a C-TPAT partner, to provide ship layout. Ship layout and most probable location of suspect cargo are provided to the cutter and COCOM via the COP.

**Knowledge**: At COCOM request, National Weather Service generates updated weather forecasts for interdiction area and provides predictions of long-range dispersion of nuclear contaminants in case of release of the IND, which is provided via the COP.

**Knowledge Development**: The vessel is interdicted in accordance with the Maritime Operational Threat Response Plan. Material is seized and the information gained provides knowledge that leads to future investigation.

**Knowledge Enablers** support every step of this process. Information architecture allows for knowledge to be disseminated across the ocean via the net-centric, common operating picture, and for data to be transmitted to analysts from space. Multi-level security allows for the sharing of knowledge across security classifications and between agencies using shared situational awareness. Without these enablers, it would be impossible to complete the knowledge cycle and achieve MDA.

Figure 2

# III. PRIORITIES

MDA is supported by cross-cutting Knowledge Capabilities that streamline the Knowledge Development process and enable the identification of Knowledge Requirements to support effective decision-making. To facilitate implementation of this plan, efforts to enhance Knowledge Capabilities or Development processes are grouped into three general priority areas: Information and Standards, Technology, and Organizations and Personnel (see Table 1). Detailed in Appendix B, these areas address identified MDA needs that support fulfillment of the MDA Essential Tasks.

| Priorities | Actions |
|---|---|
| Information and Standards | ❑ Enhance Information Collection<br>❑ Share Information<br>❑ Set Standards |
| Technology | ❑ Sensors and Platforms<br>❑ Communications<br>❑ Information Exploitation |
| Organizations and Personnel | ❑ Building Coalitions and Partnerships<br>❑ Human Intelligence Collection<br>❑ Global Maritime Community Of Interest (GMCOI) Development<br>❑ Integrated National-Level Maritime Command Centers for Maritime Operational Threat Response |

Table 1
INFORMATION AND STANDARDS

It is critical for the United States to integrate security activities with partners at home and allies abroad. To this end, the United States Government will support, develop, direct and implement policies, procedures, agreements, and standards at the international, federal, state, local and tribal levels to enhance collection, develop flexible integration systems, and provide access to information for timely support to decision-makers, operators, and first responders.

**Enhance Information Collection**

- Ensure the United States Government has greater transparency into the supply chain through industry submission of accurate, advance electronic cargo information in compliance with the Trade Act and participation in the Customs-Trade Partnership Against Terrorism (C-TPAT)

- Identify, develop, and deploy new detection and surveillance technologies across North America through the Security and Prosperity Partnership for North America

- Coordinate with international organizations to expand information requirements for data such as Advance Notice of Arrival (ANOA).

---

- Expand application of the AIS to improve the identification and tracking of marine vessels smaller than current 300 Gross Weight Tonnage (GWT) thresholds.

- Working with appropriate international organizations, ensure reservation of appropriate frequencies for use solely Automatic Identification System (AIS) users to facilitate uninterrupted data transmission to support MDA.

- Leverage national and international commercial and governmental relationships to produce dependable AIS and other vessel track reporting.

- Seek and advance agreements to enforce and expand transparency in vessel ownership.

- In the international arena, expand agreements with 'flag states' to promote accountability.

- At a national level, standardize state commercial and recreational craft registration criteria nationally; develop registration requirements for recreational boaters; and establish common vessel registration standards across federal, state and local partners.

- Expand private sector participation through joint public/private initiatives.

- Partner with willing nations to identify and monitor transnational maritime threats under existing international and domestic laws.


## Share Information

- In accordance with Executive Order 13356, "Strengthening the Sharing of Terrorism Information to Protect Amerncas," and the Intelligence Reform Act of 2004, establish legal authorities, interagency agreements, and policies to allow the processing and fusion of foreign intelligence, domestic law enforcement information, and commercial maritime data, with appropriate safeguards.

- Eliminate regulatory barriers to information sharing and interoperability through the establishment of operating protocols, memorandums of understanding and memorandums of agreement necessary for joint, interagency and industry relationships.

- Restrict access privileges to ensure data are only used for specific purpose, for finite time, and by those with necessary permissions.

- Enhance automated database, sensor, information extraction and fusion

- In compliance with law, policy, and Presidential directives, develop and implement information-handling procedures to identify data requiring special protection. Leverage current efforts to develop secure, authenticated access and user controls for classified, sensitive, or restricted information.

- Develop an open architecture for data sharing, with governance standards for web-based information storage access.

- Establish and implement interoperable communication standards, to include mandating, as appropriate, DOD's Global Information Grid (GIG) across Federal, state and local partners to enable information sharing.

- Mandate a "write-to-release" standard be applied across all collection regimes.

- Establish a network-centric, near-time virtual information grid that can be shared, at appropriate security levels, by Federal, state, local, and international agencies with maritime responsibilities. This national maritime common operating picture will be the primary means of dissemination for MDA information.

- Establish information assurance capabilities that allow the sharing of information through all levels of classification in both directions between highly classified and law enforcement sensitive sources.

## Set Standards

- Establish and gain agreement to credentialing standards for maritime port workers and mariners acceptable by Federal, state, local, and tribal authorities, based on the Transportation Worker Identification Credential (TWIC) and on the Seafarers' Identity Document (SID).

- With international partners, develop and gain agreement to credentialing standards for maritime port workers and mariners.

- Support the establishment of common biometric identification standards across the United States Government for terrorist screening.

- Continue to partner with International Standards Organization and International Maritime Organization to seek internationally recognized and accepted maritime standards and expectations of security.

### TECHNOLOGY

New capabilities to support MDA must be developed through investments in technology including sensors and platforms, communications and information sharing, and information exploitation.

## Sensors and Platforms

- Improve WMD portable and standoff detection capabilities by integrating parallel efforts. For instance, the newly created Domestic Nuclear Detection Office, charged with developing, acquiring, and supporting deployment of a domestic nuclear detection system designed to detect and report attempts to import a nuclear device or fissile and radiological material for illicit use, provides a means to seek transformational technologies.

- Bolster coastal surveillance through sensor packages, which may be shore-based, airborne, or deployed on buoys and offshore platforms, as well as shore-based and elevated integrated radar and camera (night, infrared, day) systems.

- Strengthen open ocean surveillance and reconnaissance capabilities to better verify AIS data, identify vessels not previously known, and provide additional information on crew activity, and cargo loading. Leverage commercial assets that can correlate vessel position information.

- Integrate and network existing platforms to enhance shared situational awareness. Likewise, ensure that all future acquisitions are integrated and networked with appropriate sensor technologies.

- Develop interoperability and information assurance capabilities to enable the transfer of data between sensors, platforms, and people (including assets at the lowest level) to exploit and defeat enemy vulnerabilities.

- Improve acoustic contact identification and data management.

## Communications

- Disseminate knowledge in a net-centric common operating picture, using appropriate classification levels based on information sharing standards developed in accordance with Executive Order 13356.

- Develop a common Information Technology architecture based on DOD's Global Information Grid, with an information assurance component supporting the access and sharing of information across classification boundaries

- Integrate automated vessel tracking information to improve significantly the understanding of smaller commercial and private vessel activity.

- Promote direct data transfers and electronic access to databases, intelligence files, or other repositories for inclusion in the analyzing process [e.g., National Maritime Intelligence Center databases, Treasury Enforcement Communications System (TECS), the Automated Commercial System (ACS), the Automated Targeting System (ATS), and the Automated Export System (AES)].

- Provide boarding teams the ability to identify terrorist and criminal suspects immediately through real-time connections to biometric and other identification databases and to collect biometric information.

## Information Exploitation

- Automate processes and collaborative analysis tools for collecting, fusing, and correlating structured and unstructured data to create correlated tracks and determine anomalies.

- Analyze information pertaining to vessels, cargo and people to ascertain further screening requirements and other protective measures. In a targeted assessment, data is examined to distinguish between patterns of established norms and anomalous indicators.

## ORGANIZATIONS AND PERSONNEL

To achieve MDA, organizations and personnel capabilities must provide the solid foundation for identifying the intent and understanding of threats in the maritime domain. This expanded set of coalitions, partnerships, and human intelligence collection activities builds the full-scope shared situational awareness that incorporates intelligence with law enforcement and investigative information to enable decision-making and response. To do this we must:

- Develop outreach programs to encourage members of the maritime industry and recreational boating community to report suspicious activity.

- Expand maritime community watch programs.

- Expand partnerships with allies and friends to develop and deploy new technologies such as surveillance, WMD detection, and data sharing in support of common security interests.

- Expand cooperative initiatives such as the Proliferation Security Initiative and Container Security Initiative to improve WMD interdiction in support of common security interests.

- In accordance with the Global Maritime Intelligence Integration Plan, co-locate additional maritime intelligence personnel at the National Maritime Intelligence Center. Ensure the center has the authority and connectivity to receive and merge expanded sensor data, develops computer-based algorithms to correlate threat information and generate automated alerts, and receives needed access to intelligence and national technical means.

- In accordance with the Maritime Operational Threat Response (MOTR) plan, integrate the Global Maritime Community of Interest (GMCOI) with the network of national level maritime command centers through shared situational awareness to ensure coordinated response efforts consistent with the threat identified and desired national outcome.

# IV.  Implementation

## Plan Execution

Achieving Maritime Domain Awareness requires a sustained national effort. To meet that end, the following implementation tasks are directed:

1) No later than 30 days after the effective date of this Plan, the Maritime Security Policy Coordinating Committee (MSPCC) will establish the MDA Implementation Team (MDA-IT) by approving a charter to be drafted by the Maritime Security Working Group (MSWG). The charter will specify structure and membership and will ensure coordination with all NSPD-41/HSPD-13 policy actions and plans. The MDA-IT will report to the MSPCC and coordinate implementation of this plan.

2) No later than 60 days after the effective date of this Plan, the MDA-IT will assume responsibility for all implementation actions for a period of 18 months to ensure input to one resource cycle, with subsequent renewal at the discretion of the MSPCC. The MDA Senior Steering Group (MDA-SSG) will turn over all documentation and supporting materials to the MDA-IT and dissolve, with senior policy oversight continuing at the MSPCC and NSC/HSC Deputies Committee levels.

3) The MDA-IT will:

a. Provide a forum for interagency coordination of each MDA implementation action and task, as listed in Appendix B, and others as may be subsequently identified.

b. Develop a concept of operation that will, at a minimum, detail interagency coordination, development of shared situational awareness through a national maritime common operating picture, MDA support to the Maritime Operational Threat Response Plan, and consistency with the Global Maritime Intelligence Integration Plan.

c. Recommend implementation actions to the MSPCC for each of the identified knowledge requirements.

d. Recommend policies in support of MDA to the MSPCC.

e. Recommend leads for specific MDA implementation actions and tasks to the MSPCC.

f. Ensure all MDA implementation actions and tasks are consistent with the other component plans of the NSMS.

## Resource Implications

A risk management approach will direct funding decisions across federal agencies. The MDA-IT will advise and inform departments and agencies regarding MDA resource issues, and propose a coherent, integrated interagency investment strategy. Each implementation action having resource implications will be evaluated consistent with existing departmental budgetary oversight procedures (e.g., DOD's Integrated Program

---

and Budget Review (IPBR) for DOD related elements and the Future Years Homeland Security Plan (FYHSP) for DHS related elements). The MDA-IT will ensure capability development follows the established department and/or agency acquisition and programmatic protocols [e.g., DOD/CJCS Joint Requirements Oversight Council (JROC) and Joint Capabilities Integration and Development System (JCIDS) processes, and DHS Joint Requirements Council (JRC)].

Over the long term, it is imperative that resources among the various Federal, state, local, and tribal stakeholders are complementary and provide our nation with the capabilities required to identify maritime threats. Intergovernmental organizations must work closely with the departments and agencies responsible for developing and implementing the resource plan.

## Actions

The United States Government will execute the tasks listed in Appendix B, which identifies agency level leads and actions to be taken in the near (within 2 years) and the long term (2-5 years). The actions listed are not all-encompassing, but are intended to serve as a foundation for improving MDA. The MDA-IT will evaluate additional tasks, as may be identified, and recommend leads and priority as appropriate. Specific implementation timelines and responsibilities will be developed in the course of continuing technology development and risk analysis.

# V. CONCLUSION

The United States faces a complex, dynamic strategic environment. We are engaged in a global war on terrorism with stateless actors while confronted with traditional state threats as well. These challenges to our security and economic livelihood require a new mindset – one that sees the total threat and takes all necessary actions through an active, layered defense-in-depth.

The extraordinary value of the maritime domain to global prosperity makes it an attractive medium for use by nation-states, terrorists, and other illicit elements. To achieve an active layered defense, the nation must harness or develop the means to detect illicit activities, deter our enemies from taking advantage of the maritime domain, defend United States interests at home and abroad, and defeat threats that seek to exploit our vulnerabilities as far from our shores as possible. To defeat these threats, we must achieve a more comprehensive and effective understanding of the maritime domain.

**MDA is the critical enabler that allows leaders at all levels to make effective decisions and act early against a vast array of threats to the security of the United States, its interests, allies, and friends.**

The implementation of this plan will necessarily be continuous. This *National Plan to Achieve Maritime Domain Awareness* sets forth the path toward achieving understanding of the maritime domain and ensuring its effectiveness in meeting national requirements. Achieving the capabilities called for in this plan requires the continued investment of our Nation's intellectual, technological, human and financial resources as well as a partnership with other nations.

Nothing in this plan impairs or otherwise affects the authority of the Secretary of Defense over the Department of Defense, including the chain of command for military forces from the President and Commander in Chief, to the Secretary of Defense, the command of military forces, or military command and control procedures.

# APPENDIX A: ACRONYMS AND TERMS
## ACRONYMS

| | |
|---|---|
| **ACS** | Automated Commercial System |
| **AES** | Automated Export System |
| **AIS** | Automatic Identification System |
| **ANOA** | Advanced Notice of Arrival |
| **ATS** | Automated Targeting System |
| **C-TPAT** | Customs-Trade Partnership Against Terrorism |
| **C4ISR** | Command, Control, Communication, Computers - Intelligence, Surveillance, Reconnaissance |
| **CIA** | Central Intelligence Agency |
| **CJCS** | Chairman Joint Chiefs of Staff |
| **DHS** | Department of Homeland Security |
| **DOD** | Department of Defense |
| **DOS** | Department of State |
| **DOT** | Department of Transportation |
| **FYHSP** | Future Years Homeland Security Plan |
| **GIG** | DOD's Global Information Grid |
| **GMCOI** | Global Maritime Community of Interest |
| **GMII** | Global Maritime Intelligence Integration |
| **GWT** | Gross Weight Tonnage |
| **HUMINT** | Human Intelligence |
| **IMO** | International Maritime Organization |
| **ISPS** | International Ship and Port Facility Security |
| **ISR** | Intelligence, Surveillance, and Reconnaissance |
| **JCIDS** | Joint Capabilities Integration and Development Systems |
| **JRC** | Joint Reconnaissance Center |
| **JROC** | Joint Requirements Oversight Council |
| **MDA** | Maritime Domain Awareness |
| **MOTR** | Maritime Operational Threat Response (plan) |
| **MSPCC** | Maritime Security Policy Coordination Committee |
| **NMSAC** | National Maritime Security Advisory Committee |

| | |
|---|---|
| **NSMS** | National Strategy for Maritime Security |
| **NTC** | DHS National Targeting Center |
| **SIT** | Senior Implementation Team |
| **TWIC** | Transportation Worker Identification Credential |
| **TECS** | Treasury Enforcement Communications System |
| **WMD** | Weapons of Mass Destruction |

# APPENDIX B: NEAR AND LONG-TERM PRIORITIES

| Information and Standards | | | |
|---|---|---|---|
| **Actions and Tasks** | Near Term | Long Term | Agency Lead |

### Enhance Information

| Actions and Tasks | Near Term | Long Term | Agency Lead |
|---|---|---|---|
| ☐ Ensure the United States Government has greater transparency into the supply chain through industry submission of accurate, advance electronic information in compliance with the Trade Act, and participation in the Customs-Trade Partnership Against Terrorism (C-TPAT). | X | | DHS |
| ☐ Identify, develop, and deploy new detection and surveillance technologies across North America through the Security and Prosperity Partnership for North America | | X | DOS/ DOD |
| ☐ Coordinate with international organizations to expand information requirements for data such as Advance Notice of Arrival (ANOA). | | X | DHS |
| ☐ Expand application of the AIS to improve the identification and tracking of marine vessels. | | X | DHS |
| ☐ Working with appropriate international organizations, develop a common, secure Automatic Identification System (AIS) frequency standard to facilitate uninterrupted data transmission to support MDA. | X | | DHS |
| ☐ Leverage national and international commercial and governmental relationships to produce dependable AIS and other vessel track reporting. | X | | DHS |
| ☐ Seek and advance agreements to enforce and expand transparency in vessel ownership. | X | | DHS DOT |
| ☐ In the international arena, expand agreements with 'flag states' to promote accountability and facilitate port-state control and boarding agreements. | X | X | DOS DHS |
| ☐ At a national level, standardize state commercial and recreational craft registration criteria; develop registration requirements for recreational boaters; and establish common vessel registration standards across federal, state and local partners. | X | | DHS |
| ☐ Expand private sector participation through joint public/private initiatives. | X | | DOC |
| ☐ Partner with willing nations to identify and monitor transnational maritime threats under existing international and domestic laws. | X | | DOS |

| Information and Standards | | | |
|---|---|---|---|
| **Actions and Tasks** | Near Term | Long Term | Agency Lead |
| **Share Information** | | | |
| ☐ Eliminate regulatory barriers to information sharing and interoperability through the establishment of operating protocols, Memorandums of Understanding and Memorandums of Agreement necessary for joint, interagency and industry relationships. | | X | DOD DHS |
| ☐ Restrict access privileges to ensure data are only use for specific purpose, for finite time, and by those with necessary permissions. | X | | DOD DHS |
| ☐ In accordance with Executive Order 13356 (Sharing of Terrorism Information) and the Intelligence Reform Act of 2004, establish legal authorities, interagency agreements, and policies to allow the processing and fusion and of foreign intelligence, domestic law-enforcement information, and commercial maritime data, with appropriate safeguards. | X | | DOD DHS |
| ☐ Enhance automated database, sensor, information extraction and fusion through a common distributed virtual database. | X | | DOD DHS |
| ☐ In compliance with national statutes, law, policy, and Presidential Directives, develop and implement information handling procedures to identify data requiring special protection. Leverage current Intelligence Community efforts to develop secure, authenticated access and user controls for classified, sensitive, or restricted information. | X | | DOD DHS |
| ☐ Develop an open architecture for data sharing, with governance standards for web-based information storage access. | X | | DOD |
| ☐ Establish and implement interoperable communication standards, to include mandating, as appropriate, DOD's Global Information Grid (GIG) across Federal, state and local partners to enable information sharing. | | X | DOD |
| ☐ Mandate a "write-to-release" standard be applied across all collection regimes. | X | | DOD |
| ☐ Establish a network-centric, near-real time virtual information grid that can be shared, at appropriate security levels, by Federal, state, local, and international agencies with maritime responsibilities. This national maritime common operating picture will be the primary means of dissemination for MDA information. | X | | DOD DHS |
| ☐ Establish information assurance capabilities that allow the sharing of information through all levels of classification in both directions between highly classified and law enforcement sensitive. | X | | DOD |

| Information and Standards | | | |
|---|---|---|---|
| **Actions and Tasks** | Near Term | Long Term | Agency Lead |

### Set Standards

| Actions and Tasks | Near Term | Long Term | Agency Lead |
|---|---|---|---|
| ☐ Establish and gain agreement to credentialing standards for maritime port workers and mariners acceptable by Federal, state, local, and tribal authorities, based on the Transportation Worker Identification Credential (TWIC) and on the Seafarers' Identity Document (SID). | | X | DHS |
| ☐ With international partners, develop and gain agreement to credentialing standards for maritime port workers and mariners. | | X | DHS |

| Technology | | | |
|---|---|---|---|
| **Actions and Tasks** | Near Term | Long Term | Agency Lead |

### Sensors and Platforms

| Actions and Tasks | Near Term | Long Term | Agency Lead |
|---|---|---|---|
| ☐ Improve WMD portable and standoff detection capabilities by integrating parallel efforts. For instance, the newly created Domestic Nuclear Detection Office, charged with developing, acquiring, and supporting deployment of a domestic nuclear detection system designed to detect and report attempts to import a nuclear device or fissile and radiological material for illicit use, provides a means to seek transformational technologies. | | X | DOD |
| ☐ Bolster coastal surveillance through sensor packages, which may be shore-based, airborne, or deployed on buoys and offshore platforms, as well as shore-based and elevated integrated radar and camera (night, infrared, day) systems. | | X | DHS |
| ☐ Strengthen open ocean surveillance and reconnaissance capabilities to better verify AIS data, identify vessels not previously known, and provide additional information on crew activity, cargo loading. Leverage commercial assets that can correlate vessel position information. | | X | DHS |
| ☐ Integrate and network existing platforms to enhance shared situational awareness. Likewise, ensure that all future acquisitions are integrated and networked with appropriate sensor technologies. | X | | DOD DHS |
| ☐ Develop interoperability and information assurance capabilities to enable the transfer of data between sensors, platforms, and people (including assets at the lowest level) to exploit and defeat enemy vulnerabilities. | X | | DOD DHS |
| ☐ Improve acoustic contact identification and data management. | X | | DOD |

| Actions and Tasks | Near Term | Long Term | Agency Lead |
|---|---|---|---|
| **Communications** | | | |
| ☐ Disseminate knowledge in a net-centric fashion, using appropriate classification levels based on information sharing standards developed for the Terrorism Information Sharing Environment. | | X | DOD DHS |
| ☐ Disseminate shared situational awareness via a common operating picture. | | X | DOD DHS |
| ☐ Develop a common Information technology architecture based on DOD's Global Information Grid, with an information assurance component supporting the access and sharing of information across classification boundaries. | X | | DOD DHS |
| ☐ Integrate automated vessel tracking information to improve significantly the understanding of smaller commercial and private vessel activity. | | X | DHS |
| ☐ Establish direct data transfers and electronic access to databases, intelligence files, or other repositories for inclusion in the analyzing process [e.g., National Maritime Intelligence Center databases, Treasury Enforcement Communications System (TECS), the Automated Commercial System (ACS), the Automated Targeting System (ATS), and the Automated Export System (AES)]. | | X | DOD DHS |
| ☐ Provide boarding teams the ability to identify terrorist and criminal suspects immediately through real-time connections to biometric and other identification databases and to collect biometric information. | | X | DHS |
| **Information Exploitation** | | | |
| ☐ Automate processes and collaborative analysis tools for collecting, fusing, and correlating structured and unstructured data to create correlated tracks and determine anomalies. | X | | DOD DHS |
| ☐ Analyze information pertaining to vessels, cargo and people to ascertain further screening requirements and other protective measures. In a targeted assessment, data is examined to distinguish between patterns of established norms and anomalous indicators. | | X | DHS |

| Organizations and Personnel | | | |
|---|---|---|---|
| **Actions and Tasks** | Near Term | Long-Term | Agency Lead |
| ☐ Develop outreach programs to encourage members of the maritime industry and recreational boating community to report suspicious activity. | X | | DHS |
| ☐ Expand maritime community watch programs. | X | | DHS |
| ☐ Expand partnerships with allies and friends to develop and deploy new technologies such as surveillance, WMD detection, and data sharing in support of common security interests. | | X | DOS |
| ☐ Expand cooperative initiatives such as the Proliferation Security Initiative and Container Security Initiative to improve WMD interdiction in support of common security interests. | X | X | DHS DOS |
| ☐ In accordance with the Global Maritime Intelligence Integration Plan, collocate additional maritime intelligence at the National Maritime Intelligence Center. Ensure the Center has the connectivity to receive and merge expanded sensor data, develops computer-based algorithms to correlate threat information and generate automated alerts, and receives needed access to intelligence and national technical means. | X | | DOD |
| ☐ In accordance with the Maritime Operational Threat Response (MOTR) plan, integrate the GMCOI with the network of national level maritime command centers through shared situational awareness to ensure coordinated response efforts consistent with the threat identified and desired national outcome. | X | | DOD |

The National Strategy for Maritime Security

The Maritime Infrastructure Recovery Plan

Maritime Transportation System Security Plan

National Plan to Achieve Maritime Domain Awareness

Domestic Outreach Strategy and Plan

The Maritime Commerce Security Plan

Global Maritime Intelligence Integration Plan

International Outreach Strategy to Enhance Maritime Security

Maritime Operational Threat Response Plan